D1435585

This
book belongs to

_____

...a woman who delights
in God's promises.

GROWTH AND STUDY GUIDE

Powerful Promises™ for Every Woman

Elizabeth George

HARVEST HOUSE™ PUBLISHERS

EUGENE, OREGON

Unless otherwise indicated, all Scripture quotations are taken from the New King James Version, Copyright © 1979, 1980, 1982 by Thomas Nelson, Inc., Publishers. Used by permission. All rights reserved.

Verses marked KJV are taken from the King James Version of the Bible.

Cover by Terry Dugan Design, Minneapolis, Minnesota

Acknowledgment

As always, thank you to my dear husband, Jim George, M.Div., Th.M., for your able assistance, guidance, suggestions, and loving encouragement on this project.

POWERFUL PROMISES™ FOR EVERY WOMAN GROWTH & STUDY GUIDE
Copyright © 2003 by Elizabeth George
Published by Harvest House Publishers
Eugene, Oregon 97402

ISBN 0-7369-1139-1

All rights reserved. No part of this publication may be reproduced, stored in a retrieval system, or transmitted in any form or by any means—electronic, mechanical, digital, photocopy, recording, or any other—except for brief quotations in printed reviews, without the prior permission of the Publisher.

Printed in the United States of America.

03 04 05 06 07 08 09 10 / BP-KB / 10 9 8 7 6 5 4 3 2

Contents

A Word of Welcome

❧

Please let me welcome you to this fun—and stretching!—growth and study guide for women like you who want to live out God's plan for their lives and need the help and divine enabling of His promises to do so!

A Word of Instruction

The exercises in this study guide should be easy to follow and to work. You'll need your copy of the book *Powerful Promises for Every Woman*[1] and your Bible, a pen, a dictionary, and a heart that is ready to grow. In each lesson you'll be asked to:

❦ Read the corresponding chapter from *Powerful Promises for Every Woman*.

❦ Answer questions designed to guide you to greater faith in God and greater knowledge of God.

❦ Put God's promises to work in your life as a busy, hard-pressed, and precious woman!

A Word to Your Group

Of course, you can grow (volumes!) as you work your way, alone, through these truths from God's Word and apply them to your heart. But I urge you to share the journey with other women. A group, no matter how small or large, provides personal care and adds interest. There's sharing. There are sisters-in-Christ to pray for you. There's the mutual exchange of experiences. There's accountability. And, yes, there's peer pressure—which always helps us get our lessons done! And there's sweet, sweet encouragement as together you stimulate one another to greater love and greater works of love (Hebrews 10:24).

To aid the woman who is guided by God to lead a group, I've included a section in the back of this growth and study guide called "Leading a Bible Study Discussion Group."

A Word of Encouragement

What a wonderful, rich surprise awaits you as you open this book that is focused on twelve precious and powerful promises from the Bible, promises that have carried Christians for literally thousands of years through every day and every difficulty of their lives.

Do you have difficulties? Are your days hard and long, full and challenging? Then God has promises for you—and every woman—as you look to Him for help. Dip into God's heavenly pool of promises. Find strength in His wisdom and peace, His tender love and His ever-present care and comfort...and above all, His power. Please, enjoy the enabling promises for every day, minute, and step of your journey through life. Enjoy God's promises to you!

God's Promises for You

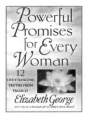

> He will feed His flock
> like a shepherd.
> —ISAIAH 40:11

In your personal copy of *Powerful Promises for Every Woman* read the opening chapter titled, "God's Promises for You." Make notes here about what meant the most to you from this chapter or offered you the greatest challenge or strengthened your trust in God.

~ God's Truths ~

As we begin to learn more about God's promises for every woman, read Psalm 23 in your Bible. "The Shepherd Psalm" is a familiar Psalm, so familiar, in fact, that it's easy to rush through it without paying attention to its fullness and the richness of its language and the scope of its many powerful promises. Make this time of reading special.

The Seasons of Your Life

1. I shared about the seasons of my life. Now take a few minutes to share about yours.

2. What truth is taught and what promise is made in Psalm 23:4 regarding all the seasons, years, even the minutes, of your life?

    How does it comfort and/or encourage you to know this promise—that the Lord is "with" you through all the seasons of life (Psalm 23:4)?

3. On this subject of the presence of God, what did David, the inspired writer of Psalm 23, also say in Psalm 16:8?

    And what does Isaiah 43:2 say on the same subject?

    And Isaiah 41:10?

Dear one, He is with you! As one has said, at every point—and season, even at the "point of danger," God is "alongside to escort. In times of need, companionship is good."[2] And you, my friend, have the companionship of the Lord God!

The Psalmist

Whenever I'm deciding whether or not to purchase a book, I always read the back-cover copy or the book's dust jacket. I want to find out as much as I can about the author. I want to know what qualifies him or her to write on the subject matter of the book. It's also true that knowing something about the author helps me as the reader to better understand that person's work.

With this in mind, let's find out about David, the person God used to bring us Psalm 23 with its many marvelous promises. Let's read David's bio, his biographical information, and learn more about the seasons of his life. Check out the scripture verses listed to see what God tells us about David.

1. We first meet David in 1 Samuel 16. Where was David when Samuel came to anoint him to be king (16:11)?

    Where was he when Saul needed a musician (16:19)?

    And where was he when his father needed him to take supplies to his brothers (1 Samuel 17:20)?

2. David was probably a teenager when he faced the giant, Goliath. How did his experience as a shepherd help him to fight a giant (17:34-36)?

    What shepherd implements did David use against Goliath (17:40)?

3. When God called David to lead His people, what did He say to him in 2 Samuel 5:2?

    And in 2 Samuel 7:8?

4. Describe David's leadership role according to Psalm 78:70-72.

The Psalmist's Seasons

We learned about David's seasons of youth, maturity, and leadership. But we also discovered that David's great faith in a great God carried him through...

> ...a season of rejection,
>
> ...a season of fear,
>
> ...a season of discouragement,
>
> ...a season of disappointment, and
>
> ...a season of heartbreak.

And now for you, dear one. How does *David's great faith* in God encourage and strengthen you in your seasons? Take a minute or two to jot down some specifics here.

And how do *David's great failures* encourage and instruct you in your seasons? Again, jot down some specifics here.

~ A Moment with the Shepherd ~

♪ How do you think David's early career as a shepherd shaped and prepared him to lead God's people?

Can you think of ways that God has used your past to shape your present? (And have you thanked Him?)

❧ How did the prophet Samuel describe David (1 Samuel 13:14; see also Acts 13:22)?

Write out what you think it means to be "a woman after God's own heart" and make your answer a matter of prayer.

❧ David was a man of great faith. But he was also a man of great failure. And beloved, this is true of everyone! So, how are you handling your failures? Do you perhaps need to admit any past or current sins? What did David say happens when you and I (and David!) admit our sins (Psalm 51:3,7-14)? Make a list...and the longer the better!

Or maybe you've suffered. This, too, is true of everyone. According to 2 Corinthians 1:3-4, how does God help His children when they suffer?

Or maybe you need to "go on" after your failure and suffering. Read for yourself the sobering scene described in 2 Samuel 12:13-20 and David's efforts to go on. What steps can you take today to rise up and go on after any disobedience or hard times?

How does Philippians 3:13-14 help?

And how about 2 Corinthians 4:8-9?

And Philippians 4:13?

As we end our time of getting acquainted with David, the psalmist, and learning about the seasons of his life, consider these eloquent words from author Charles Swindoll regarding the seasons of life.

A Word About the Seasons of Life

Each of the four seasons offers fresh and vital insights.... As each three-month segment of every year holds its own mysteries and plays its own melodies... so it is in the seasons of life. The Master is neither mute nor careless as He alters our times and changes our seasons. How wrong to trudge blindly and routinely through a lifetime of changing seasons without discovering answers to the new mysteries and learning to sing the new melodies! Seasons are designed to deepen us, to instruct us in the wisdom and ways of our God. To help us grow strong....[3]

1

God's Promise of Care

The LORD is my shepherd.
—PSALM 23:1

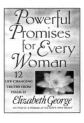 In your personal copy of *Powerful Promises for Every Woman* read about Promise #1, "God's Promise of Care." Make notes here about what meant the most to you from this chapter or offered you the greatest challenge or strengthened your trust in God.

~ God's Truths ~

The Bible contains many references to God as our Shepherd. In fact, the phrase "the Lord is my shepherd" is a name of God—*Jehovah-Rohi*. Let's look now at some scriptures that describe the Lord as a shepherd.

Jehovah-Rohi Feeds, Leads, and Warns

1. Notice these references to sheep and shepherds from the Psalms:

Psalm 74:1—How does the psalmist view God's people?

Psalm 77:20—How does the psalmist view God's guidance?

Who were two of God's shepherds?

Psalm 78:52-53—Again, how does the psalmist view God's people?

And God's guidance?

Psalm 79:13—Once more, how does the psalmist view God's people?

Psalm 80:1—How does the psalmist address God?

2. Now look at Isaiah 40:11. What role and actions does Isaiah ascribe to God?

3. Moving to the New Testament, note some of its references to shepherds:

   John 10:11-16,26-28—Who is speaking?

   How does He refer to Himself (verses 11,14)?

   Hebrews 13:20—How is Jesus referred to here?

   1 Peter 2:25—And here?

   1 Peter 5:4—And here?

   Revelation 7:17—And here?

   What new assurances do you enjoy when you realize that Jesus is your Shepherd?

4. Now note from John 10 the characteristics of Jesus'
    sheep:

    Verse 4–

    Verse 5–

    Verse 14–

    Verse 27–

    Verse 28–

~ A Moment with the Shepherd ~

Now that you know more about the role of a good shepherd and His care for His own...

❧ Think about Jehovah-Rohi, about how He *feeds* us. How's your appetite for God's food, for His Word? Please describe your times in God's Word—in God's green pastures—this past week.

God promises to care for you, and His care involves faithfully feeding you. What adjustments do you need to make in your "feeding" habits? How can you alter your daily schedule to allow for time to "feed" on God's Word?

🔊 Think about Jehovah-Rohi, about how He *leads* us. How's your willingness to follow? Do you balk? Hesitate? Follow grudgingly? Blatantly refuse? Or do you enjoy trusting in God and "following hard" after Him (see Psalm 63:8 KJV)? Answer honestly.

Again, God promises to care for you, and His care involves faithfully leading you. Is there anything God is asking of you today that you are failing to heed and to follow? Are there any adjustments you need to make in your "following" habits?

§   Think about Jehovah-Rohi, about how He *warns* us. God
     warns us because He wants the best for us. His standards
     are meant to protect us. Are any warning lights flashing
     in your life? Any alarms going off? Are you playing life
     too close to the edge? Are you dabbling in areas of sin? Is
     the path your life is taking one of heeding God's warnings
     against folly and judgment? Please explain.

Again, God promises to care for you, and His care
involves faithfully warning you. He warns us through His
Word and by the conviction of sin prompted by His Holy
Spirit (John 16:8). Are you partaking of things God
explicitly warns you against? Or are you involved in any
activities that are not honoring and pleasing to Him? Are
there any adjustments you need to make in your "listening" habits? Any things that must be radically elimi-
nated from your life? Please explain.

§ Think back on the beautiful description of God in Isaiah 40:11. What are the fears you face today?

And how do these words about God's care for you "comfort you" (as Isaiah 40:1 says)?

§ Look again at your answers from John 10. As you consider the behaviors that characterize the sheep that follow Jesus, which ones cause you to evaluate your own "following"?

§ Also read again the descriptions of the restless and discontent sheep, the worldling sheep, and the devoted sheep. Now answer the question, "Which of these three kinds of sheep am I?" Please explain.

Again, do you have any corrections to make in your "following" habits? List them here.

Write out a plan of action and a prayer of commitment to be a more devoted follower.

§   Finally, note here the sacrifice of the Good Shepherd on your behalf (John 10:11,15).

In view of Jesus' willingness to sacrifice His life for you, what steps will you take to be a more committed and obedient follower?

How blessed we are to have a God who cares about us, His women, *and* to have the care of our God! The extent of God's promise to care for His own is unmeasurable, unsearchable, and fathomless. Yet here's a sample listing of God's care of and for you from the Bible. Read that list now. And don't fail to look up these powerful promises in your Bible. Mark them, put them to work, and memorize them. And, of course, don't fail to thank Jehovah-Rohi!

$\mathscr{A}$ *Word About God's Promises*

✓ God will "keep" you as the apple of His eye (Psalm 17:8).

✓ He will "keep" you in all your ways (Psalm 91:11).

✓ He will "keep" you in perfect peace (Isaiah 26:3).

✓ He will "keep" that which you have committed to Him against that day (2 Timothy 1:12).

✓ He will "keep" you from the hour of temptation and support you in the time of trial (1 Corinthians 10:13).

✓ He will "keep" you from falling (Jude 24).

✓ He will "keep" you as a shepherd cares for his flock of sheep (Jeremiah 31:10).[4]

2

God's Promise of Provision

❧

I shall not want.
—Psalm 23:1

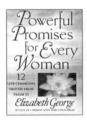

In your personal copy of *Powerful Promises for Every Woman* read about Promise #2, "God's Promise of Provision." Make notes here about what meant the most to you from this chapter or offered you the greatest challenge or strengthened your trust in God.

~ God's Truths ~

One of my favorite Christian songs is "All That I Need Is All That You Are." Not only is the song lovely and the lyrics inspiring, but the title seems to say it all when it comes to the person of God and His provision of the "needs" of every one of His women.

As we think about the essential needs in life, it's comforting to have the promise of God's provision so that we may confidently declare, "I shall not want," and realize that all that we need is all that He is! God's provision for us illustrates another character trait of the Lord as revealed in His name *Jehovah-Jireh*, "The Lord will provide."

Meet Jehovah-Jireh

1. Quickly read through Genesis 22:1-14, which tells the story of Jehovah-Jireh.

   Who are the principal people (verses 1 and 2)?

   What was God's command (verse 2)?

   What was the problem (verse 7)?

   What answer was given (verse 8)?

   What was God's solution (verse 13)?

   What name was given to the place where this occurred (verse 14)?

2. Both Abraham and his wife, Sarah, had a long history of trusting God...and of *learning* to trust God! Look now to the New Testament to find out more about their trust in Jehovah-Jireh. As you read, remember that Hebrews 11 has been given such titles as "The Saints' Hall of Fame," "The Honor Roll of Old Testament Saints," and "Heroes

of Faith."[5] Note the instances and the details of faith in God as revealed in…

…Abraham in Hebrews 11:8-10–

…Sarah in Hebrews 11:11–

…Abraham and Sarah's offspring in Hebrews 11:12-13–

…Abraham in Hebrews 11:17-19–

3. Now that we've noted the faith of Sarah, read about her encounter with the Lord in Genesis 18:1-15.

   What announcement did the Lord make in verse 10?

   And what was Sarah's response (verses 10-15)?

   And why (verses 11-13)?

   What searing question did the Lord ask Sarah—and you!—in verse 14?

4. What is said of Abraham's faith in Romans 4:20-21?

God Provides

1. Did you catch what the apostle Paul said in Romans 4 about Abraham's faith in "the promises of God"? Look now at these scriptures and note the promises made and the conditions for these promises.

                             Promise   Condition

    Psalm 34:9–

    Psalm 34:10–

    Psalm 84:11–

2. Truly God promises to meet the needs of His people! Note several more instances of God's provision.

    Deuteronomy 2:7—How long had God met His people's needs?

Deuteronomy 8:7-9—What did God promise His people in the Promised Land?

~ A Moment with the Shepherd ~

§ I shared some items on my "list of life's needs." Now it's your turn. Jot down what you consider to be the primary necessities in life.

Now write down the promise from Psalm 23:1.

For an additional blessing, look again at the remainder of Psalm 23. Then list the many "needs" God promises to meet.

§ Jehovah-Jireh! Think back now on the command God gave to Abraham in Genesis 22:2. What do you think you would have done?

§   Now think back on Sarah's encounter with the Lord in Genesis 18. As you think about your faith in God and your responses to your problems and to His promises, what answer do you think you are exhibiting in response to God's question to Sarah in verse 14, "Is anything too hard for the LORD?"

Can you think of any seemingly impossible situation you're now experiencing?

How does the thought of Jehovah-Jireh—"the LORD will provide"—encourage you?

~ ❧ ~

A Word About God's Promises

Beloved, hear now this well-loved story that has been passed down through the years. It seems that...

Once upon a time there was a dear woman of faith who loved the Lord and believed in His "exceedingly great and precious promises" (2 Peter 1:4). When this lady died, she willed her tattered and worn-out Bible to her favorite nephew. Her will simply stated, "I bequeath my family Bible and all it contains."

Like many young people, the nephew set the Bible aside and went on with life. Not once did he bother to open it.

The days and decades came and went...and so did the nephew's trials and tribulations. Finally, after years of poverty, the nephew was once again packing his belongings because he was—once again—being forced to move due to a lack of funds. As he tossed his belongings into a box, he found the musty old Bible. Casually, he fanned the pages with his thumb. As he did so, something inside caught his eye, causing him to open up the Bible to see what was there. It was then he discovered a bank note made out to him, worth many thousands of dollars! The treasure had been tucked away in the Bible for most of his life while he went without.

Dear one, God has bequeathed us our Bible. Let us not live an impoverished Christian life. Let's open God's Word and enjoy the wealth and provision of His promises to us. As He has promised, we "shall not want."

~ ~ ~ ❧ ~ ~ ~

Another Word About God's Promises

"I shall not want." Let not those fear starving that are at God's finding and have him for their feeder. More is implied than is expressed, not only, *I shall not want*, but, "I shall be supplied with whatever I need; and, if I have not every thing I desire, I may conclude it is either not fit for me or not good for me or I shall have it in due time."[6]

3

God's Promise of Rest

❧

He makes me to lie down in green pastures.
—PSALM 23:2

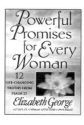 In your personal copy of *Powerful Promises for Every Woman* read about Promise #3, "God's Promise of Rest." Make notes here about what meant the most to you from this chapter or offered you the greatest challenge or strengthened your trust in God.

~ God's Truths ~

David, the writer of Psalm 23, was a shepherd, and his language reflects his time as a shepherd with his sheep in the hill country of Judah. Let's find out now how this imagery of lying down in green pastures relates to our need for rest.

The Place of Rest

1. Quickly note how these references describe "green pastures."

Deuteronomy 32:2–

2 Samuel 23:4–

Proverbs 27:25–

How would these conditions contribute to the rest of
   sheep?

2. Now look at these scriptures that refer to the physical
   "resting places" of sheep.

2 Samuel 7:8–

Isaiah 65:10–

and of sheep and camels—Ezekiel 25:5–

and of God's people—Isaiah 32:18–

In your own words, what seems to be pictured in these
   images?

The Plan for Rest

1. According to Exodus 20:10, what is God's purpose for the Sabbath?

2. Jesus, too, knew of man's need for rest and planned for it. How does Mark 6:30-32 reveal this?

3. And what do these verses indicate about Jesus' physical needs?

   Mark 4:38–

   John 4:6–

The Procedure for Rest

1. According to Psalm 23:2, what is God's procedure for ensuring rest for His own?

2. The prophet Elijah was one of God's choice servants who was assigned by God to prophesy a long, extended drought to King Ahab (1 Kings 17:1). When Elijah next saw King Ahab, it resulted in a showdown between God and His representative, Elijah, and the priests of Baal (1 Kings 18:20-40). At this point, Queen Jezebel threatened Elijah's life, and he began to run. Let's pick up the story of God's care for Elijah in 1 Kings 19.

How distraught was Elijah (verses 1-5)?

How did God minister to Elijah (verses 5-6)?

And how did He minister to him again in verse 7?

And what was the result of Elijah's rest and God's provision and care for him (verse 8)?

One more thing—how else did God tend to and encourage His faithful, tired prophet (verses 9-21)? Take your time. God ministered to Elijah in many ways!

~ A Moment with the Shepherd ~

⑤   Take a minute to think about the times when you need rest. What is your mental condition?

And your physical condition?

And your spiritual condition?

How does a time of resting in the presence of the Lord refresh you?

✆ Think again about the three conditions mentioned in your book that interfere with the rest every woman needs to live out her many daily duties and responsibilities— fear, hunger, and fighting. Then look at these promises, assurances, and instructions in your Bible. How do they contribute to your rest and peace?

Fear—First consider Isaiah 41:10. How does God promise to fortify you?

What does God promise in the following verses?

Joshua 1:9–

Deuteronomy 31:6–

Exodus 33:14–

Psalm 3:5 and 4:8–

Hunger—"God's ordinances are the green pastures in which food is provided for all believers; the word of life is the nourishment of the new man. It is milk for babes, pasture for sheep...a green pasture for faith to feed in."[7]

Do a heart check: Answer the following questions simply and then share what you plan to do about your condition.

Do you consider your times in God's Word a *necessity?*

Do you enjoy the nourishment of God's Word *regularly?*

Is your appetite for God's Word growing *increasingly?* (And which stage best describes your times in God's Word—the cod liver oil stage, the shredded wheat stage, or the peaches and cream stage?)

Fighting—Describe your internal emotions and their physical effects on you when you are involved in an argument, quarrel, or dispute, or when you witness it between others. How does the elimination or solution of the problem bring rest?

❧ Does it comfort you to know that the Lord "makes" you lie down in green pastures and rest? I shared about a time when God "made" me lie down in His green pastures. Now, can you share a time from your life? How did God "make" you rest? How did He provide it?

And what were the results?

❧ "Waiting" can become one of God's opportunities for rest for His busy and breathless and sometimes beat-up sheep!

How do you think waiting creates an opportunity to learn to trust the Lord?

How do you think waiting causes you to grow in patience?

How do you think waiting encourages and creates greater fellowship with God?

How do you think waiting energizes you for the day—or days—ahead?

What can you do today to "lie down" in God's "green pastures" and experience His promised rest?

A Word About God's Promises

It's been said that there are three primary positions for handling life's difficulties—struggling, clinging, and resting.

The classic illustration for these three positions is that of a shipwreck when people are thrown into the sea and fighting for their lives.

> In the *struggling* position they are in the water, fighting with the waves, and are in need of help themselves.

> In the *clinging* position they are holding on to the lifeboat; they are quite safe themselves, but cannot help anyone else, because both their hands are holding on for dear life!

> In the *resting* position they are sitting in the lifeboat with both hands free to help others.

God promises to give you rest, not only for the nourishment and strength that comes to yourself, but also for what your invigorated life can do for others. The goal of every woman should be to grow beyond struggling and clinging to the position of *resting in the Lord* so that she is able to help others.

4

God's Promise of Peace

❦

He leads me beside the still waters.
—PSALM 23:2

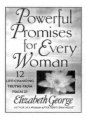 In your personal copy of *Powerful Promises for Every Woman* read about Promise #4, "God's Promise of Peace." Make notes here about what meant the most to you from this chapter or offered you the greatest challenge or strengthened your trust in God.

~ God's Truths ~

The Lord who is our Shepherd knows our need for peace. Therefore He promises to lead us to places—like the still waters—to ensure that we drink in, take in, and bask in His peace.

"He Leads Me..."

Note how these scriptures show us how the Lord leads us:

Psalm 77:20–

Isaiah 40:11–

Isaiah 49:10–

"…Beside the Still Waters"

There's no doubt that every woman has a need for peace as she attempts to live her busy life in a hectic world. However, throughout time God's people have found their "still waters," their "place," for tapping into God's peace. Note the places (or Person) where these people of God found peace.

Abraham in Genesis 19:27–

David in Psalm 32:7–

The psalmist in Psalm 119:114–

Daniel in 6:10–

Mary in Luke 10:39–

Jesus in Mark 1:35–

Jesus in Luke 22:39-41–

Meet Jehovah-Shalom and Gideon

Jehovah-Shalom! Quickly read through Judges 6:11-24, where Jehovah-Shalom—the name of God meaning "Jehovah is peace"—is first introduced.

How did the Angel of the Lord greet Gideon (verse 12)?

What did the Angel of the Lord ask of Gideon (verse 14)?

Why was Gideon so disturbed (verse 15)?

How did the Lord calm Gideon's fears (verse 16)?

What caused Gideon to fear for his life again (verse 22)?

And what was the Lord's answer (verse 23)?

And how did Gideon commemorate this encounter with God (verse 24)?

The Promise of Peace

God's peace is also promised to you in the New Testament. What new information do you learn from these verses?

John 14:27—

Romans 5:1—

1 Corinthians 14:33—

2 Thessalonians 3:16—

Peace from Following God

Did you relate to the story of my friend and her struggle with "the four **A**'s"? Look now at what God's Word says about each of the "**A**'s." And while you're working through this exercise, ask your heart if there is anything you are failing to do to follow God.

Any thing—Acts 9:6–

Any where—Isaiah 6:8–

Any time—Matthew 2:13-14–

At any cost—Philippians 3:7-8–

How does Abraham's obedience to God in Genesis 12:1 and 4 demonstrate the four **A**'s?

~ A Moment with the Shepherd ~

Have you made a "transaction" with Jehovah-Shalom, the Prince of Peace? If not, why not? And why not now?

If so, recount briefly how you became a Christian.

§   What hurdle are you now facing? And what fears do you have regarding your future? How does it encourage you to know that the Lord, your Shepherd, "leads" you every step of the way through life?

And how does it encourage you to know that God leads you to places of peace "beside still waters"?

How does the fact that the Lord is with you strengthen your courage and give you peace to face what you know is coming…and what you don't know is coming—the known and the unknown?

§   Do you have a time and "a place" where you retreat regularly to commune with the God of peace? Describe them here.

My time is…

My place is…

❧ As you think about "the four **A's**," is there any area in your life where you are failing to follow God's leading? And can you pinpoint why? Are there fears? Worries? Anxieties? Is there disobedience? Why not ask God to give you His strength to commit to follow Him as He "leads" you so that you may experience His perfect peace?

❧ After learning more about God's promise of peace, can you think of *any* instance when you should not enjoy God's peace? Please explain your answer.

How do you plan to use the truths learned in this lesson to help you fight against fear or worry and gain God's peace? Be specific.

Isn't it reassuring to have the promise of God's peace? How *could* we as busy women make it through life—even through one day of life!—without it? But God is faithful to lead us to a place of peace, at least in our hearts, if not in our surroundings. God's peace is promised and available...if we would but follow our Shepherd. So, dear one, *walk* with God. Then you will experience God's peace!

~ § ~

A Word About God's Promises

One of the most revered of divine titles to Jew and Christian alike is Jehovah-Shalom, "the Lord is peace" (Judges 6:24). That He is the God of Peace is seen in the fact that this attribute dominates the Bible. Definite and implied promises on the many aspects of this theme abound. To gather together all the references to "peace" provides one with an antidote for fear, unrest, and turmoil in times like these. Run your eye over these "peace" texts, and your song will be–

> Peace, peace, sweet peace,
> Wonderful gift from above;
> Oh, wonderful, wonderful peace,
> Sweet peace, the gift of God's love.

The Lord give thee peace (Numbers 6:26) and bless his people with peace (Psalm 29:11).

Great peace have they that love thy law (Psalm 119:165).

All His paths are peace (Proverbs 3:17).

He is our peace (Ephesians 2:14), the Prince of Peace (Isaiah 9:6), will keep you in perfect peace (Isaiah 26:3).

Let the peace of God rule in your hearts (Colossians 3:15).[8]

~ ~ ~ § ~ ~ ~

5

God's Promise of Healing

He restores my soul.
—PSALM 23:3

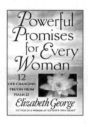 In your personal copy of *Powerful Promises for Every Woman* read about Promise #5, "God's Promise of Healing." Make notes here about what meant the most to you from this chapter or offered you the greatest challenge or strengthened your trust in God.

~ God's Truths ~

What woman doesn't need her soul restored? And what woman doesn't need her spirit healed? Do you ever feel the need for a spiritual repair job? Then take heart! Your Shepherd sees to that need too!

1. According to Hebrew scholars, the restoration of the "soul" in Psalm 23:3 means the rekindling or quickening of the exhausted spirit. To find more definitions, use an

English dictionary to look up a few simple meanings of the word "restore" and jot them here:

2. Now that you have a better idea of the concept of restoration, look in your Bible at these references to healing and restoration—both physical and spiritual—and note the need in each instance.

Psalm 19:7–

Psalm 23:3–

Psalm 51:12–

Psalm 147:3–

Isaiah 61:1–

Jeremiah 3:22–

Jeremiah 27:22–

Jeremiah 30:17–

    a.

    b.

Galatians 6:1–

The Character of Jehovah-Rophe

Jehovah-Rophe! Here is yet another name of God—Jehovah-Rophe (meaning "Jehovah heals")—that teaches us more about His ministry of healing and restoration. What great event in Israel's history is related in Exodus 14:27-31?

How did the Israelites respond (15:1)?

According to 15:22-23, what was the first trial God's people faced in the wilderness?

And how did they respond (verse 24)?

What was God's solution (verse 25)?

List the four requirements God laid out for His people (verse 26).

1.

2.

3.

4.

What did God promise to do if these four conditions were met (verse 26)?

Finally, how did God refer to Himself (verse 26)?

The Case of Elijah

As we've already learned in our study, Elijah was one of God's cast-down sheep. List here "The Course of Restoration" from your book.

Stage 1–

Stage 2–

Stage 3–

Read again 1 Kings 19. Note these three stages of restoration in Elijah's cast-down condition. How did God "heal" and restore His beloved prophet and servant?

Stage 1–

Stage 2–

Stage 3–

Promises from the New Testament

God's "restoration" is also emphasized in the New Testament. As you look at these verses, list the concerns of and for the saints. (And don't fail to notice that the emphasis is on *spiritual* restoration rather than on *physical* restoration.)

Paul's prayer in Ephesians 1:15-18–

Paul's prayer in Ephesians 3:14-19–

Paul's prayer in Philippians 1:9-11–

Paul's prayer in Colossians 1:9-12–

John's greeting to his "beloved Gaius" in 3 John 2–

~ A Moment with the Shepherd ~

§ How do you generally respond to physical or emotional testing? Or how would someone close to you say that you generally respond to physical or emotional testing?

What spiritual responses does God desire from you, regardless of your physical condition?

§ As you think about God's promise in Psalm 23:3 to heal and restore your broken heart and crushed spirit and to bind up your wounds (see Psalm 147:3), what better response will you give to testing in the future?

§ What encouragement do you receive from God's restoration of His prophet Elijah in 1 Kings 19:4-15?

And what practical lessons do you learn...

...about taking care of your physical and spiritual condition?

...about ministering to others?

❧   What actions can you take to ensure spiritual health and "healing" in the two areas of...

...feeding on God's Word?

...communing with God through prayer?

❧   Jot down a plan of action that will help you look to God to rekindle and quicken your soul the next time you are down or discouraged or suffering physically.

Healing. Just hear the word and we immediately think of physical healing, don't we? Our physical health is definitely important, especially when it's deteriorating! But oh, how encouraging it is to know that God is more concerned for our spiritual health and promises to strengthen us spiritually for the physical trials that will most assuredly come our way. Though outwardly we are wearing down and wasting away, inwardly we are being restored and renewed day by day (2 Corinthians 4:16).

Dear one, rather than giving up or giving in to weakness, weariness, and depression, let us look up—up to God and to His high and treasured promises. Let God give us His promised strength to deal with the inevitable and trust Him to work out the impossible.

A Word About God's Promises

Your adversary would love for you to assume the worst about your situation. He would enjoy seeing you heave a sigh and resign yourself to feelings of depression. However...when God is involved, anything can happen. The One who directed that stone in between Goliath's eyes and split the Red Sea down the middle and leveled that wall around Jericho and brought His Son back from beyond takes delight in mixing up the odds as He alters the inevitable and bypasses the impossible.[9]

6

God's Promise of Guidance

*He leads me in the paths
of righteousness for His name's sake.*
—PSALM 23:3

In your personal copy of *Powerful Promises for Every Woman* read about Promise #6, "God's Promise of Guidance." Make notes here about what meant the most to you from this chapter or offered you the greatest challenge or strengthened your trust in God.

~ God's Truths ~

God not only leads us as His women beside His still waters and restores our souls, He also promises to guide us in the paths of righteousness.

Desiring to Walk with God

As a child of God (and a sheep of the Shepherd!), your desire should be to follow His guidance. See what you can learn from these scriptures about that desire.

1. What does the psalmist cry out for in Psalm 16:11?

   And in Psalm 27:11?

2. And what does the psalmist say will help him to stay on the path (Psalm 119:105)?

The "Paths of Righteousness"

The word "path" is also translated "way" in the Bible. What do you learn from these verses?

Proverbs 12:15–

Proverbs 31:27–

Isaiah 30:21–

Isaiah 55:8-9–

Walking in God's Paths

1. Our Shepherd faithfully guides us, but we have choices to make about our following. What do these references teach you about following the Shepherd's guidance?

    Psalm 119:30–

    Psalm 119:59-60–

    Proverbs 3:6–

2. Read now Proverbs 4:14-15 and itemize the six specific instructions God gives us for walking in righteousness and staying on His righteous path.

    1–

    2–

    3–

    4–

5–

6–

3. Now read Proverbs 4:23-27 and itemize the specific instructions God gives us in each verse for walking in righteousness and staying on His righteous path.

   Verse 23–

   Verse 24–

   Verse 25–

   Verse 26–

   Verse 27–

   Proverbs 23:19–

The God of Righteousness—Jehovah-Tsidkenu

1. According to Psalm 23:3, why does God guide us in the paths of righteousness?

2. *Jehovah-Tsidkenu!* Here is yet another name of God. The name Jehovah-Tsidkenu (meaning "the Lord our righteousness") reveals the righteousness of God to us and His standard of righteousness.

   As we look into the history of this name of God, we learn that God's people had continually sinned against Him for more than 100 years before being taken captive. Obviously they needed help in meeting God's standard. What was God's solution (Jeremiah 23:5-6)?

   What promise from God would this future event fulfill from 2 Samuel 7:16?

God's Guidance in the New Testament

As New Testament believers we receive help from God to walk in His paths of righteousness. What do you learn from these scriptures about some of God's means of helping us?

John 16:13–

Galatians 6:1–

James 1:5–

Hebrews 13:17–

~ A Moment with the Shepherd ~

§   Evaluate "the path" of your life. Are you walking in God's "stiff and straight" path of righteousness? Please explain your answer.

Are there any areas where you have strayed off the path of righteousness? Please, be honest.

Look again and list below the seven **A**'s that quickly turn
our bad habits and wrong ways into a righteous walk.

A

A

A

A

A

A

A

Now, determine if you are weak in any of these practices.
If so, which ones? Check or circle them, and explain.

What will you do today to remedy any problem?

§   We are constantly bombarded by other "voices," and it's possible you may be listening to those "voices" instead of to God's. What are some of those voices, according to these verses?

1 Corinthians 15:33–

Galatians 5:16–

1 John 2:15–

Now look again at Psalm 119:30. God *promises* to guide you as His woman. Do you perhaps need to spend more time in God's Word looking at His "stiff and straight" ordinances and being guided by Him?

What plan of action could you make…and take?

♫ "For His name's sake" is an important reason for God's guidance of you, His child. Now, how can you more rigorously guard *your* family's reputation? How can you more faithfully watch over the *ways*—the paths—of your loved ones (Proverbs 31:27)?

♫ And speaking of "for His name's sake," what can you do today to be more careful to guard your Shepherd's name and reputation?

♫ Before you enjoy the poetry below, check your heart once again. Read again the four "heart-check" questions at the end of your chapter. Pray along with David in Psalm 139:23-24 and search your heart.

> *Search me, O God, and know my heart;*
> *Try me, and know my anxieties;*
> *And see if there is any wicked way in me,*
> *And lead me in the way everlasting.*

Now, dear one, do what you must to benefit from God's promise to guide you *as* you obediently follow Him! It doesn't matter *where* God is leading and guiding you. It only matter that *He* is your Guide, and that He *is* leading you, and that He is leading you in *His* paths of righteousness.

A Word About God's Promises

He does not lead me year by year
Nor even day by day,
But step by step my path unfolds;
My Lord directs the way.

Tomorrow's plans I do not know,
I only know this minute;
But He will...say, "This is the way,
By faith now walk ye in it."

And I am glad that it is so,
Today's enough to bear;
And when tomorrow comes, His grace
Shall far exceed its care.

What need to worry then or fret?
The God who gave His Son
Holds all my moments in His hand
And gives them, one by one.[10]

7

God's Promise of Presence

❧

Yea, though I walk through
the valley of the shadow of death,
I will fear no evil;
for You are with me.
—PSALM 23:4

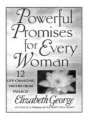 In your personal copy of *Powerful Promises for Every Woman* read about Promise #7, "God's Promise of Presence." Make notes here about what meant the most to you from this chapter or offered you the greatest challenge or strengthened your trust in God.

~ God's Truths ~

Suddenly our walk through God's promises turns from green pastures, still waters, and paths of righteousness... down into the valley of the shadow of death. Every woman has traveled or will travel down into the "valley of the shadow." Let's see how God's promises can assist you and me as we travel this new path with Him.

The Way of the Path

1. There's no better way to grasp the meaning of "the valley of the shadow of death" than to look at some of its uses in the Bible. So, quickly note these uses and any other descriptive words used with the phrase "shadow of death."

   [Example] Job 3:5—darkness, cloud, blackness [What does your Bible say?]

   Job 10:21-22–

   Job 16:16–

   Job 24:17 (two times)–

   Job 28:3–

   Job 34:22–

   Job 38:17–

Psalm 44:19–

Psalm 107:10,14–

Jeremiah 2:6–

Jeremiah 13:16–

2. In ten words or less, summarize the meaning of "shadow of death."

The Walk on the Path

1. We love Psalm 23 and its peaceful, pastoral beauty. But leading sheep was a dangerous profession. David, the author of Psalm 23, knew what it was like to walk daily with the sheep. What had he experienced along the way (1 Samuel 17:34-36)?

2. In Genesis 31:38-40 Jacob details what it was like to shepherd the flocks of Laban. What were some of the dangers and drudgeries?

3. Describe the gruesome scene pictured in Amos 3:12.

4. And, according to Luke 2:8, what was another duty of shepherds?

God's Presence on the Path

1. Even with the dangers of the shadow of death, why was the psalmist not afraid (Psalm 23:4)?

2. Other Old Testament scriptures speak of the promise of God's presence. What do these few reveal?

    Deuteronomy 31:6–

    Joshua 1:9–

    Psalm 46:1-2–

    Isaiah 41:10–

3. The New Testament is filled with promises of the presence of God. What do these scriptures promise?

    Matthew 28:20–

    Acts 18:9-10–

    Hebrews 13:5-6–

~ A Moment with the Shepherd ~

☙ Clearly shepherding had its dangers and terrors. Every shepherd and his flock spent time in "the valley of the shadow of death." And so do we. Can you share a time when you faced a particularly dark and difficult situation?

How did the promise of God's presence help you at that time?

☙ When you think about the future, is there anything you dread? Why?

How does the promise of God's presence dispel these fears?

And how does David's famous "I will" from Psalm 23:4 help you with the temptation to fear?

§ Every woman faces trials and tragedies, difficulties and discouragements. As you face any current difficulties, are you looking to the Lord, counting on His promised presence, and refusing to fear? Share briefly.

What three commands does Jesus give in John 14:1?

—

—

—

How are you doing in the trust department? And what can you do to increase your trust in God and His promises?

Why not memorize a verse on fear to help you rest in the promise of God's presence? Look again at the promises regarding fear and the presence of God in chapter 3, page 56. Pick one, write it here, hide it in your heart, and…fear not!

ᔓ Finally, what does Jesus say is the role of the Holy Spirit in our lives today (John 14:16-17)?

ᔓ In your book I shared that at all times—even in your dark times—you…

…walk by divine appointment,

…walk in divine presence,

…walk by divine grace, and

…walk by divine purpose.

Beloved, these statements are true, whether you believe it or not. But…imagine how your "walk" with God through hard times would be enriched by remembering that you walk by divine appointment, in God's promised presence, by His all-sufficient grace, and according to His divine purpose!

It's also true that the more lofty our thoughts about God, the better we are able to cope with the issues of life. Write out how your attitude would improve in any current trials by remembering these lofty thoughts about God.

A Word About God's Promises

We value the promise by the character of him that makes it. We may therefore depend upon God's promises; for good and upright is the Lord, and therefore he will be as good as his word. He is so kind that he cannot deceive us, so true that he cannot break his promise. Faithful is he who hath promised who also will do it. He was good in making the promise, and therefore will be upright in performing it.[11]

8

God's Promise of Comfort

✍

> *I will fear no evil;*
> *for You are with me.*
> *Your rod and Your staff,*
> *they comfort me.*
> —PSALM 23:4

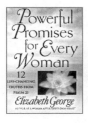 In your personal copy of *Powerful Promises for Every Woman* read about Promise #8, "God's Promise of Comfort." Make notes here about what meant the most to you from this chapter or offered you the greatest challenge or strengthened your trust in God.

~ God's Truths ~

In our last lesson we learned what it means to walk through "the valley of the shadow of death." We also acknowledged that every woman will walk through that dark valley. But...we also learned about the wonderful promise of God's presence in that valley of darkness from David's words, "I will fear no evil; for You are with me."

Jehovah Is There

1. *Jehovah-Shammah!* This name of God—meaning "Jehovah is there"—should bring you much comfort as you walk with God throughout all of life. God had promised His presence among His people from the beginning. Note some of the manifestations of His presence:

Exodus 23:20–

Exodus 40:34-38–

2 Chronicles 7:1-3–

But then something happened, something terrible! What happened due to the desecration of God's temple by God's people (Ezekiel 10:18)?

What is the final promise for the new heaven and earth (Ezekiel 48:35)?

Hear now these words regarding Jehovah-Shammah in Ezekiel 48:35:

"The city is called YHWH [Jehovah] Shammah, 'The LORD is there.'" The departed glory of God...has returned... and His dwelling, the temple, is in the very center of the district given over to the Lord. With this final promise, all of the unconditional promises which God had made to Israel in

>   the Abrahamic Covenant (Genesis 12),
>   the Levitic Covenant (Numbers 25),
>   the Davidic Covenant (2 Samuel 7), and
>   the New Covenant (Jeremiah 31)

have been fulfilled. So this final verse provides the consummation of Israel's history—the returned presence of God![12]

2. Take another minute or two and note what these verses say about God's presence:

Psalm 46:1–

verses 4-5a–

verse 7–

verse 11–

Psalm 132:13-14–

Isaiah 12:6–

Isaiah 63:9–

Jeremiah 3:17–

This was a lot of information to take in, but it's important to know a little about the history of the presence of God with His people.

Comfort Is There

1. When David acknowledged God's presence in Psalm 34:4, what effect did it have upon him?

2. Who are the people who enjoy God's comfort in Psalm 34:18?

3. And in Psalm 145:18?

4. As a New Testament believer, you have another source of help and comfort. What Person of God is always present with you according to these scriptures?

   John 14:17–

1 Corinthians 3:16–

1 Corinthians 6:19–

5. Regarding comfort, what promises, truths, and benefits do you discover in 2 Corinthians 1:3 and 4? (Don't forget to notice that God's comfort is active, extensive, purposeful, and specific!)

The Rod and the Staff Are There

In addition to God's marvelous presence, you also have the presence of His weapons—His rod and His staff—to comfort you. Note some of the uses of these two weapons.

Genesis 49:10–

Exodus 21:19–

Leviticus 27:32–

2 Samuel 7:14–

2 Samuel 23:21—

Micah 7:14—

Zechariah 8:4—

As you can readily see, these two implements had a variety of uses. In the imagery of Psalm 23, you can also sense the comfort and confidence the rod and the staff would bring not only to the shepherd, but also to the sheep.

~ A Moment with the Shepherd ~

Comfort! What woman doesn't need it...and need it daily! And yet we have all the comfort we need in the presence of God, who is near to all who believe in Him and belong to Him.

§   How does the knowledge of the Shepherd's weapons and His ability to use them on your behalf comfort you? And in what specific situations?

§   How does God use them to protect you?

To correct you?

To guide you?

To dispel your fears?

     As you think about your day, your week, the year ahead, and the path of the future, how does the promise of God's presence comfort you? After writing out your answer, thank God for His presence and care "thru ev'ry day, o'er all the way."[13] Then enjoy this sublime poetry that points our hearts to God's promised presence in our lives for all our todays and all our tomorrows.

A Word About God's Promises

Fear thou not for I am with thee,
I thy God—be not dismayed:
Face the days that lie before thee,
Trust Me and be unafraid.

When the nights are darkest trust Me;
Trust Me when the days are bright.
'Tis My mighty hand upholds thee,
Though 'tis hidden from thy sight.

All the journey I am with thee,
All thy weakness I'll sustain;
Never shall My presence leave thee:
Trust Me still in joy and pain.

Trust Me when the shadows lengthen,
And the shades of night draw near;
I am with thee still to strengthen.
Trust in Me and have no fear.

When for thee life's journey's ended
And thy days of service o'er—
With Me Who for thee has tended
Thou shalt be for evermore.[14]

9

God's Promise of Friendship

❦

You prepare a table before me
in the presence of my enemies;
You anoint my head with oil;
My cup runs over.
—Psalm 23:5

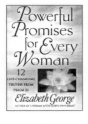 In your personal copy of *Powerful Promises for Every Woman* read about Promise #9, "God's Promise of Friendship." Make notes here about what meant the most to you from this chapter or offered you the greatest challenge or strengthened your trust in God.

~ God's Truths ~

Eastern hospitality! Some say there's nothing like it. Let's learn a little more about what it meant to be a guest in a Middle Eastern home or tent at the time Psalm 23 was written...and how as one of God's women you can extend hospitality and friendship to many.

The Server and the Supply

1. Look at the scene of the gracious hosts, Abram and Sarai, in Genesis 18:1-8. Make note of the preparations they made for their guests. As you write out your answers, also note what related to the *server*, what related to the *supply*, and what related to the *style*.

    Eagerness (verse 2)–

    Posture (verse 2)–

    Attitude (verse 3)–

    Provision (verse 4)–

    Menu (verses 6-8)–

    Preparation (verses 6-7)–

    Presentation (verse 8)–

2. Now look in on the scene in Genesis 19:1-3. What similarities do you notice? Again, note the information about the *server*, the *supply*, and the *style*.

   Verse 1–

   Verse 2–

   Verse 3–

3. Consider, too, "the wise woman" from Proverbs 9:1-6. She sets a model of hospitality for every woman! What was a part of her work (verse 2)? Once again, what described the *server*, the *supply*, and the *style*?

   What kind of attitude did she exhibit toward hospitality (verse 3)?

4. A few scenes of hospitality and friendship in the Holy Land from the New Testament reveal its same importance. As usual, pay attention to the *server*, the *supply*, and the *style*.

Who extended the loving care and service of hospitality in John 13:2-5?

And to whom?

And in John 21:12-13?

And to whom?

Lydia was a woman who extended hospitality and friendship to many. Who were the recipients of her graciousness in Acts 16:14-15 and 40, and what did she offer?

Aquila and Priscilla were a couple who continually opened their hearts and their home to others. To whom—and in what ways—did they extend their gracious hospitality and friendship in...

...Acts 18:1-3–

...Romans 16:3-5–

...1 Corinthians 16:19–

Mary, the mother of John Mark, also opened her heart and home to others. To whom, and for what purpose, according to Acts 12:12?

5. What does the New Testament say to you in this vital area of hospitality and friendship with other believers?

Romans 12:13–

Hebrews 13:2–

1 Peter 4:9–

A Sample of Blessings

List the ten blessings cited in your book that you enjoy as a child of God and that are available to you. As you write your list, make notes regarding your personal pattern of hospitality toward others. You may also want to share a memory of when such a blessing was offered to you by someone else!

Blessing 1–

Blessing 2–

Blessing 3–

Blessing 4–

Blessing 5–

Blessing 6–

Blessing 7–

Blessing 8–

Blessing 9–

Blessing 10–

~ A Moment with the Shepherd ~

§ Think about your own family and your opportunities to minister to their physical and spiritual needs at the table. Then read over the ten blessings that are characteristic of a visit in the Lord's tent. Now, rate yourself as the *server*.

Also rate your *supply* and the *style* in which you serve your loved ones.

How could you better make the time spent at your table an intimate feast in the wilderness of the world and a festival of joy? (I've left a rather large space, so write your heart out. And don't forget to make some changes!)

 ❧ As you take in these warm and generous and gracious instances of friendship to strangers, or "stranger love" (the meaning of hospitality), what do you conclude about hospitality?

About mealtime?

About meal preparations?

Can you think of two or three changes you need to make in the area of hospitality?

 ❧ Read again my quote from this chapter's facing page (page 136) in your book. Can you say that family and guests experience these same blessings as they step into your house? Why, or why not?

Dear sister, I have read countless surveys that identify the number-one problem women face as loneliness. Most of the women who report this as a pressing problem are either single and have no close friends, or they are married to husbands who are distant either by design or because of the demands of work.

But for a Christian woman, loneliness should be only a fleeting issue. Why? Because we have a friend who is always there—Jesus—whom we can always talk to and visit with.

Now, think about this: Your hospitality—your open heart and open home—is a way that you extend the care and friendship you enjoy with Jesus to others.

A Word About God's Promises

This Shepherd Psalm as a whole reveals the Shepherd's ability to care for us in every way. If we are His sheep and His private mark is upon us, then we know that because of His kind, tender, and generous heart all our fears are follies, our forebodings are sinful, and our anxieties groundless, for He is able to "supply all our needs, according to his glorious riches in Christ Jesus."[15]

10

God's Promise of Protection

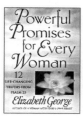

...in the presence of my enemies;
—PSALM 23:5

In your personal copy of *Powerful Promises for Every Woman* read about Promise #10, "God's Promise of Protection." Make notes here about what meant the most to you from this chapter or offered you the greatest challenge or strengthened your trust in God.

~ God's Truths ~

Wasn't it exciting to look at the picture of generous hospitality portrayed in Psalm 23:5? Now let's consider the setting for this gracious provision—"in the presence of my enemies"—and the protection the host promises his guests.

The Situation

1. To refresh yourself about the scene spoken of in Psalm 23:5, what was the situation and the setting described for the weary pilgrim's feast?

2. Meet Ezra. This godly man was preparing to begin a pilgrimage from Babylon back to Jerusalem.

   What did Ezra do for protection before he began his trek (Ezra 8:21)?

   Why (verse 22)? (Be careful—it's a multiple answer!)

   How did God answer Ezra's prayer for protection (verses 23 and 31)?

3. Those who entered an Eastern home were promised protection by the host at all costs. You can observe this fact in Joshua 2:1-6. Briefly note the host and the guest(s) and a few details surrounding their safety.

The Scene

1. *A scene of warm hospitality*—Describe again the lavish provisions listed in Psalm 23:5.

   Review again the story of Lot's hospitality to his guests in Genesis 19.

   Describe his attitude (verse 1).

   Describe his invitation (verse 2).

   When the angels declined, how did Lot persist (verse 3)?

   Once his guests were inside, what did Lot do (verse 3)?

2. *A scene of security*—Continuing on in the account of Lot's hospitality to two angels, what happened after dinner (verse 4)?

What did the people want (verse 5)?

What did Lot do about the situation in verses 6-7?

In verse 8?

What next happened to Lot (verse 9)?

In your own words how far was Lot willing to go to protect his guests?

3. *A scene of victory*—As your book stated, sometimes a prisoner was chained to the pillars of a palace and forced to "feast" his eyes on a victory feast. In Judges 16:23 who was celebrating?

How did they celebrate (verse 25)?

The Savior—Jehovah-Nissi

1. Even when there is no home or host in sight, you have the Lord to protect you from your enemies. This protection is

provided by *Jehovah-Nissi*——meaning "Jehovah, my banner." Look now to Exodus 17 for the history of this great name of God.

What was happening in this scene (verse 8)?

How did Moses respond (verse 9)?

What was Moses' role (verse 9)?

How did the battle go (verses 11-12a)?

And how was the problem solved (verse 12)?

And what was the result (verse 13)?

How did Moses respond to this (verse 15)?

2. How do you think Moses interpreted the victory of the Israelites?

And why?

3. *Nissi*, or standard, or banner, was a pole with an emblem placed on top of it. For a better understanding of the use of a banner, look at Numbers 21.

    What was the problem (verses 5-6)?

    What did God tell Moses to do (verse 8)?

    And what was the result (verse 9)? Or, how were those who looked at the banner or bronze-serpent ensign on the pole protected?

Several Promises of Protection

1. Note now a few of the many ways God protects you as His dear child. And...good news! Some of them are promises!

    Proverbs 18:10–

    Psalm 3:5 and 4:8–

Psalm 27:1–

Psalm 34:7–

Psalm 121:7-8–

John 10:28-29–

2. And, by the way, God has also given you armor for protection. Read Ephesians 6:10-17.

What commands are given to you in verses 10-11?

What are the six most necessary pieces of spiritual armor with which God equips His children to resist and overcome Satan's assaults?

Verse 14–

Verse 14–

Verse 15–

Verse 16–

Verse 17–

Verse 17–

As you can see, God's promises to protect extend to every man and every woman who believe in, belong to, and obey Him!

~ A Moment with the Shepherd ~

ð   Can you think of a favorite promise from the Bible that has reminded you of God's protection? Write it here and also record the situation that brought it to your mind.

֍ And can you think of a time when you experienced a victory or "won a battle" in the presence of your enemies because God's banner was over you? Again, supply a few details.

֍ Spend a few minutes going over the truths of Psalm 139:1-12 that affirm that you are never out of the protective presence of the Lord—even when you're in the presence of your enemies! For which of these truths are you most thankful? And why?

As we end this time of learning about Jehovah-Nissi, I can't resist mentioning the many times (and maybe you did the same thing!) I have sung the familiar chorus, "His Banner over Me Is Love." What a wonderful banner of protection God's love is! God loved the world and sent His Son (John 3:16). Christ loved the church and died for her (Ephesians 5:25). And Jesus loves me, and nothing can separate me from that love (Romans 8:38-39). What a marvelous protection God's banner of love is, for me...*and* for you!

A Word About God's Promises

For all the promises of God
in Him are Yes, and in Him Amen.
—2 Corinthians 1:20

The promises of God comprise to the believer an armory, containing all manner of offensive and defensive weapons. Blessed is he who has learned to enter into the sacred arsenal, to put on the breastplate and the helmet, and to lay his hand to the shield and to the sword![16]

11

God's Promise of Hope

🌿

Surely goodness and mercy
shall follow me
all the days of my life
—PSALM 23:6

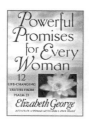

In your personal copy of *Powerful Promises for Every Woman* read about Promise #11, "God's Promise of Hope." Make notes here about what meant the most to you from this chapter or offered you the greatest challenge or strengthened your trust in God.

~ God's Truths ~

The final verse of Psalm 23! And what a verse it is! David makes a turn in his thinking...from what God does and has done for him...to what God will do for him...forever.

Looking Backward...and Upward

In your book I shared about "The Box" that I found in my closet at home. It was a little metal box filled with documents that indicated someone (in my case, my husband) had been taking care of me...and planned to take care of me in the future.

Well, dear one, Psalm 23 is "The Ultimate Box" for every woman! In it we find evidence that Someone—God!—has indeed been taking care of our every need up to this very present minute today. Look back over Psalm 23 and note all that God promises to provide for His people through life.

Verse 1–

Verse 2–

Verse 3–

Verse 4–

Verse 5–

Moving from Experience to Faith

Now note what God promises to provide for His own in the future. Then we'll examine more closely these powerful and assuring promises that bring us hope.

Verse 6a–

Verse 6b—

Seven Reasons for Hope in the Future
~Part 1~

This final verse of Psalm 23 brings us a panoramic view of life. It also brings us seven reasons for confidence and hope for the future.

1. God's Continued Goodness

Goodness is one of God's attributes and a grace He promises to His people. Read now about an amazing scene between God and His servant Moses described in Exodus 33:12-23. As you can see, Moses needed hope and assurance!

What was Moses' request in verse 18?

Why (verses 12-17)?

What was God's response to His timid servant (verse 19)?

And in Exodus 34:6?

What do you learn about God's goodness from the verse above?

And from Psalm 31:19?

And from Psalm 100:5?

2. God's Continued Mercy

Mercy is another of God's attributes and another of His graces that He promises His people will enjoy. Read the following scriptures. What do you learn about God's mercy and the hope that His mercy brings?

Exodus 33:18-19 and 34:6–

Psalm 100:5–

Psalm 103:4–

Lamentations 3:22-23–

Titus 3:5–

3. God's Continued Pursuit

David explains that God's goodness and mercy will "follow" him. These two solid, dependable qualities of the Lord will most assuredly "follow after" and "pursue" and "accompany" David. How vigorously? As vigorously as David's enemies pursued him throughout his life!

How would this promise bring hope to David's life?

And to yours?

4. God's Continued Presence

And how long does David say that God's goodness and mercy will pursue him?

How would this promise bring hope to David's life?

And to yours?

~ A Moment with the Shepherd ~

§ Throughout our walk with the Shepherd in Psalm 23 we've focused on what we consider to be our "needs" and God's gracious provision for those needs. Think now of any *present* difficulties you are dealing with. Make a note of them here.

How does the thought of God's goodness and mercy provide hope and encouragement in these trials?

§ Think, too, of any *future* problems you are likely to encounter between now and the time you enter "the house of the Lord." List several here.

How does the thought of God's goodness and mercy encourage you as you think about these problems?

❧ Jesus commanded, "Do not worry about your life...." (Matthew 6:25). Take a minute to evaluate yourself in this area of worry and anxiety over the daily demands and circumstances of life. How would you rate yourself on the worry scale? How is your behavior when it comes to obeying this command from the Bible?

How will David's statement of hope ("Surely goodness and mercy shall follow me all the days of my life") help you to comply with Jesus' charge in Matthew 6:25?

And Matthew 6:34?

Dear one, for you and me as Christian women, "hope" is not to be seen as an uncertainty. We are not "hoping" that God's promises will come true. No, we rather have "confident hope" in God's promises, for we have confidence in the character of God. A promise is only as good as the one who makes the promise. So, because of God's goodness and mercy, we have a confident hope for all the days of our lives—and beyond—"through Jesus Christ our Savior" (Titus 3:6).

A Word About God's Promises

The multitudinous promises—"eighty-five for each day of the year," one writer computes—cover all our needs, whether for the body, home, mind and soul, and for the whole of life, both here and hereafter. These wonderful promises fit our varied needs as the key fits the lock, and we can never find ourselves in any situation without an appropriate promise. Our petitions for temporal, physical, and spiritual blessings should be as detailed and specific, as were the experiences of the saints of old.[17]

12

God's Promise of Home

❦

*And I will dwell
in the house of the LORD forever.*
—PSALM 23:6

In your personal copy of *Powerful Promises for Every Woman* read about Promise #12, "God's Promise of Home." Make notes here about what meant the most to you from this chapter or offered you the greatest challenge or strengthened your trust in God.

~ God's Truths ~

Just mention the word "home" and a woman's mind tends to race toward decorating, organizing, and cleaning. She thinks about the nest she's creating for her loved ones. And magazines like *House Beautiful* and *Better Homes and Gardens* quickly come to mind. But let's look at what the Bible says about "home."

Seven Reasons for Hope in the Future
~Part 2~

As we begin to wrap up not only Psalm 23:6 but the whole of Psalm 23, review your previous lesson and its corresponding chapter in your book. Then note here the first four "Reasons for Hope in the Future" before we continue on.

1.

2.

3.

4.

And now let's examine our final three reasons for hope.

5. Eternal Worship

The desire to worship God resides at the core of every believer's heart and soul. We adore our God and yearn to express that adoration. Our souls long to praise Him, and our lips long to join in joyful praise, thanksgiving, gladness, singing, and prayer.

David wrote, "...and I will dwell in the house of the Lord forever." Throughout his life, David longed for God and longed to be with God. His words expressed a deep desire for the continual presence of God and the realization of constant communion with Him. What can we learn about the house of the Lord and about David's desires from these words written by him?

Psalm 26:8–

Psalm 27:4–

What did others write about *the house of the* LORD?

Psalm 84:4–

Psalm 100:3 and 4–

6. Eternal Home

The writer of Psalm 23 (and of special note, verse six), David-the-shepherd and David-the-fugitive, spent much of his life on the move.

How and where did David live a great deal of his life?

1 Samuel 22:1–

1 Samuel 24:1-3–

1 Samuel 26:1-3–

2 Samuel 15:27-28–

How does the psalmist refer to himself in Psalm 119:19?

And how does Peter refer to all Christians in 1 Peter 2:11?

And what does Jesus tell us about "home" (John 14:2-3)?

7. Eternal Presence

The greatest blessing in every believer's life—man or woman—will be that of eternal, intimate fellowship with God, in His presence, forever. We live for it, we long for it, and we look forward to it.

🖢 How does Psalm 84:1-2 express the longings of the soul for God's eternal presence?

🖢 And how does Revelation 21:3-4 explain God's eternal presence and our experience in His presence?

🖢 What (or Who!) awaits us in heaven, according to Hebrews 8:1?

Eternal worship, an eternal home, and eternal presence! We, above all creatures, are most blessed by these divine promises! David desired the fullness of joy and the forevermore pleasures of the Lord's presence in a forevermore home. And the same is true of you and me.

~ A Moment with the Shepherd ~

It's obvious as David closes Psalm 23 with *the house of the Lord* in mind that he was consumed with God and with the thought of enjoying an eternal home with Him.

🖢 How do you think these practices would help you to be "consumed" with the Lord, and how do you think they would better prepare you to be with God forever?

Matthew 6:19-21—

Colossians 3:1—

Colossians 3:2—

Hebrews 10:25—

§   Meet Anna. She was a woman who desired eternal wor-
    ship, an eternal home, and the eternal presence of God.
    She is also a woman who teaches us *how* to be consumed
    with God. As you read her story now in Luke 2:36-38,
    keep in mind that Anna was probably a woman who had
    no kin.

    How did Anna choose to live out the days of her earthly
    existence? And which of the three reasons for hope did
    this choice fulfill?

    Where did Anna choose to live out the days of her earthly
    existence? And which two of the three reasons for hope
    did this choice fulfill?

What did Anna do that instructs you on what it means to be consumed in the here and now with God while you wait for the hereafter?

Now, what do you plan to do to live more like Anna and to be more consumed with God and His promises?

🔥 Look again at Revelation 21:3-4. What about this scene causes you to yearn for a home in heaven?

🔥 Give an honest answer to this question: Exactly how deeply do you long for heaven?

And what can you do to move your desires closer to David's desire to dwell in the house of the Lord forever?

🔥 Of the 12 promises described in Psalm 23, which one or ones give you the greatest assurance as you face the future?

God's promises for every woman! We've touched, tasted, and handled 12 of them, *twelve* of God's "exceedingly great and precious promises" (2 Peter 1:4)!

It's true that these 12 promises from Psalm 23 are promises for a lifetime. But, dear one, there are more—more promises available to you as you trek through life. Estimates of the number of promises in the Bible range from 8,810 to 30,000.[18] And every one of them, regardless of who received the promise, is built upon the person and character of God.

~ § ~

A Word About God's Promises

Every promise is built upon four pillars:

God's justice and holiness, which will not suffer Him to deceive;

His grace and goodness, which will not suffer Him to forget;

His truth, which will not suffer Him to change; and

His power, which makes Him able to accomplish.[19]

~ ~ ~ § ~ ~ ~

Leading a Bible Study Discussion Group

❧

What a privilege it is to lead a Bible study! And what joy and excitement await you as you delve into the Word of God and help others to discover its life-changing truths. If God has called you to lead a Bible study group, I know you'll be spending much time in prayer and planning and giving much thought to being an effective leader. I also know that taking the time to read through the following tips will help you to navigate the challenges of leading a Bible study discussion group and enjoying the effort and opportunity.

The Leader's Roles

As a Bible study group leader, you'll find your role changing back and forth from *expert* to *cheerleader* to *lover* to *referee* during the course of a session.

Since you're the leader, group members will look to you to be the *expert* guiding them through the material. So be well prepared. In fact, be over-prepared so that you know the material better than any group member does. Start your study early in the week and let its message simmer all week long. (You might even work several lessons ahead so that you have in mind the big picture and the overall direction of the study.) Be ready to share some additional gems that your group members wouldn't have discovered on their own. That extra insight from your study time—or that comment from a wise Bible teacher or scholar, that clever saying, that keen observation from another believer, and even an appropriate joke—adds an element of fun and keeps Bible study from becoming routine, monotonous, and dry.

Next, be ready to be the group's *cheerleader*. Your energy and enthusiasm for the task at hand can be contagious. It can also stimulate people to get more involved in their personal study as well as in the group discussion.

Third, be the *lover*, the one who shows a genuine concern for the members of the group. You're the one who will establish the atmosphere of the group. If you laugh and have fun, the group members will laugh and have fun. If you hug, they will hug. If you care, they will care. If you share, they will share. If you love, they will love. So pray every day to love the women God has placed in your group. Ask Him to show you how to love them with His love.

Finally, as the leader, you'll need to be the *referee* on occasion. That means making sure everyone has an equal opportunity to speak. That's easier to do when you operate under the assumption that every member of the group has something worthwhile to contribute. So, trusting that the Lord has taught each person during the week, act on that assumption.

Expert, cheerleader, lover, and referee—these four roles of the leader may make the task seem overwhelming. But that's not bad if it keeps you on your knees praying for your group.

A Good Start

Beginning on time, greeting people warmly, and opening in prayer gets the study off to a good start. Know what you want to have happen during your time together and make sure those things get done. That kind of order means comfort for those involved.

Establish a format and let the group members know what that format is. People appreciate being in a Bible study that focuses on the Bible. So keep the discussion on the topic and move the group through the questions. Tangents are often hard to avoid—and even harder to rein in. So be sure to focus on the answers to questions about the specific passage at hand. After all, the purpose of the group is Bible study!

Finally, as someone has accurately observed, "Personal growth is one of the by-products of any effective small group. This growth is achieved when people are recognized and accepted by others. The more friendliness, mutual trust, respect, and warmth exhibited, the more likely that the member will find pleasure in the group, and, too, the more likely she will work hard toward the accomplishment of the group's goals. The effective leader will strive to reinforce desirable traits" (source unknown).

A Dozen Helpful Tips

Here is a list of helpful suggestions for leading a Bible study discussion group:

1. Arrive early, ready to focus fully on others and give of yourself. If you have to do any last-minute preparation, review, re-grouping, or praying, do it in the car. Don't dash in, breathless, harried, late, still tweaking your plans.

2. Check out your meeting place in advance. Do you have everything you need—tables, enough chairs, a blackboard, hymnals if you plan to sing, coffee, etc.?

3. Greet each person warmly by name as she arrives. After all, you've been praying for these women all week long, so let each VIP know that you're glad she's arrived.

4. Use name tags for at least the first two or three weeks.

5. Start on time no matter what—even if only one person is there!

6. Develop a pleasant but firm opening statement. You might say, "This lesson was great! Let's get started so we can enjoy all of it!" or "Let's pray before we begin our lesson."

7. Read the questions, but don't hesitate to reword them on occasion. Rather than reading an entire paragraph of instructions, for instance, you might say, "Question 1 asks us to list some ways that Christ displayed humility. Lisa, please share one way Christ displayed humility."

8. Summarize or paraphrase the answers given. Doing so will keep the discussion focused on the topic, eliminate digressions, help avoid or clear up any misunderstandings of the text, and keep each group member aware of what the others are saying.

9. Keep moving and don't add any of your own questions to the discussion time. It's important to get through the study guide questions. So if a cut-and-dried answer is called for, you don't need to comment with anything other than a "thank you." But when the question asks for an opinion or an application (for instance, "How can this truth help us in our marriages?" or "How do *you* find time for your quiet time?"), let all who want to contribute do so.

10. Affirm each person who contributes, especially if the contribution was very personal, painful to share, or a quiet person's rare statement. Make everyone who shares a hero by saying something like "Thank you for sharing that insight from your own life," or "We certainly appreciate what God has taught you. Thank you for letting us in on it."

11. Watch your watch, put a clock right in front of you, or consider using a timer. Pace the discussion so that you meet your cut-off time, especially if you want time to pray. Stop at the designated time even if you haven't finished the lesson. Remember that everyone has worked through the study once; you are simply going over it again.

12. End on time. You can only make friends with your group members by ending on time or even a little early! Besides, members of your group have the next item on their agenda to attend to—picking up children from the nursery,

babysitter, or school; heading home to tend to matters there; running errands; getting to bed; or spending some time with their husbands. So let them out *on time!*

Five Common Problems

In any group, you can anticipate certain problems. Here are some common ones that can arise, along with helpful solutions:

1. *The incomplete lesson*—Right from the start, establish the policy that if someone has not done the lesson, it is best for her not to answer the questions. But do try to include her responses to questions that ask for opinions or experiences. Everyone can share some thoughts in reply to a question like, "Reflect on what you know about both athletic and spiritual training and then share what you consider to be the essential elements of training oneself in godliness."

2. *The gossip*—The Bible clearly states that gossiping is wrong, so you don't want to allow it in your group. Set a high and strict standard by saying, "I am not comfortable with this conversation," or "We [not *you*] are gossiping, ladies. Let's move on."

3. *The talkative member*—Here are three scenarios and some possible solutions for each.

   a. The problem talker may be talking because she has done her homework and is excited about something she has to share. She may also know more about the subject than the others and, if you cut her off, the rest of the group may suffer.

   SOLUTION: Respond with a comment like: "Sarah, you are making very valuable contributions. Let's see if we can get some reactions from the others," or "I know Sarah can answer this. She's really done her homework. How about some of the rest of you?"

b. The talkative member may be talking because she has *not* done her homework and wants to contribute, but she has no boundaries.

SOLUTION: Establish at the first meeting that those who have not done the lesson do not contribute except on opinion or application questions. You may need to repeat this guideline at the beginning of each session.

c. The talkative member may want to be heard whether or not she has anything worthwhile to contribute.

SOLUTION: After subtle reminders, be more direct, saying, "Betty, I know you would like to share your ideas, but let's give others a chance. I'll call on you later."

4.   *The quiet member*—Here are two scenarios and possible solutions.

a. The quiet member wants the floor but somehow can't get the chance to share.

SOLUTION: Clear the path for the quiet member by first watching for clues that she wants to speak (moving to the edge of her seat, looking as if she wants to speak, perhaps even starting to say something) and then saying, "Just a second. I think Chris wants to say something." Then, of course, make her a hero!

b. The quiet member simply doesn't want the floor.

SOLUTION: "Chris, what answer do you have on question 2?" or "Chris, what do you think about...?" Usually after a shy person has contributed a few times, she will become more confident and more ready to share. Your role is to provide an opportunity where there is *no* risk of a wrong answer. But occasionally a group member will tell you that she would rather not be called on. Honor her request, but from time to time ask her privately if she feels ready to contribute to the group discussions.

In fact, give all your group members the right to pass. During your first meeting, explain that any time a group member does not care to share an answer, she may simply say, "I pass." You'll want to repeat this policy at the beginning of every group session.

5. *The wrong answer*—Never tell a group member that she has given a wrong answer, but at the same time never let a wrong answer go by.

> SOLUTION: Either ask if someone else has a different answer or ask additional questions that will cause the right answer to emerge. As the women get closer to the right answer, say, "We're getting warmer! Keep thinking! We're almost there!"

Learning from Experience

Immediately after each Bible study session, evaluate the group discussion time using this checklist. You may also want a member of your group (or an assistant or trainee or outside observer) to evaluate you periodically.

May God strengthen—and encourage!—you as you assist others in the discovery of His many wonderful truths.

Notes

1. Elizabeth George, *Powerful Promises for Every Woman* (Eugene, OR: Harvest House Publishers, 2000).

2. Derek Kidner, *The Tyndale Old Testament Commentaries—Psalms 1-72* (Downers Grove, IL: InterVarsity Press, 1978), p. 111.

3. Charles R. Swindoll, *Growing Strong in the Seasons of Life* (Grand Rapids, MI: Zondervan Publishing House, 1983), p. 15.

4. Roy B. Zuck, *The Speaker's Quote Book* (Grand Rapids, MI: Kregel Publications, 1997), p. 170.

5. John MacArthur, *The MacArthur Study Bible* (Nashville: Word Publishing, 1997), p. 1916.

6. Matthew Henry, *Commentary on the Whole Bible—Volume 3* (Peabody, MA: Hendrickson Publishers, 1996), p. 258.

7. Ibid.

8. Herbert Lockyer, *All the Promises of the Bible* (Grand Rapids, MI: Zondervan Publishing House, 1962), p. 25.

9. Charles R. Swindoll, *The Tale of the Tardy Oxcart* (Nashville: Word Publishing, 1998), p. 263.

10. Zuck, *The Speaker's Quote Book*, quoting Barbara G. Ryberg, p. 182.

11. William T. Summers, compiler, *3000 Quotations from the Writings of Matthew Henry* (Grand Rapids, MI: Fleming H. Revell, 1982), p. 233.

12. MacArthur, *The MacArthur Study Bible*, p. 1224.

13. Hymn by Civilla D. Martin, "God Will Take Care of You."

14. A. Naismith, *A Treasury of Notes, Quotes and Anecdotes,* poem by J. C. Whitelaw (Grand Rapids, MI: Baker Book House, 1976), p.185.

15. Lockyer, *All the Promises of the Bible*, p. 155.

16. D. L. Moody, *Notes from My Bible and Thoughts from My Library*, quoting C. H. Spurgeon (Grand Rapids, MI: Baker Book House, 1979), pp. 276-77.

17. Lockyer, *All the Promises of the Bible*, p. 155.

18. Ibid., p. 10.

19. Zuck, *The Speaker's Quote Book*, quoting H. G. Salter, p. 320.

Personal Notes

Personal Notes

Personal Notes

Personal Notes

Personal Notes

Personal Notes

Personal Notes

≈ ≈ ♪ ≈ ≈

Personal Notes

Personal Notes

About the Author

Elizabeth George is a bestselling author and speaker whose passion is to teach the Bible in a way that changes women's lives. For information about Elizabeth's books or speaking ministry, to sign up for her mailings, or to share how God has used this book in your life, please write to Elizabeth at:

Elizabeth George
P.O. Box 2879
Belfair, WA 98528

Toll-free fax/phone: 1-800-542-4611
www.elizabethgeorge.com

Books by Elizabeth George

Beautiful in God's Eyes—The Treasures of the Proverbs 31 Woman
Life Management for Busy Women
Loving God with All Your Mind
Powerful Promises™ for Every Woman—12 Life-Changing Truths from Psalm 23
A Woman After God's Own Heart®
A Woman After God's Own Heart® Deluxe Edition
A Woman After God's Own Heart® Audiobook
A Woman After God's Own Heart® Prayer Journal
A Woman's High Calling
A Woman's Walk with God
A Young Woman After God's Own Heart

Growth and Study Guides

Life Management for Busy Women Growth & Study Guide
Powerful Promises™ for Every Woman Growth & Study Guide
A Woman After God's Own Heart® Growth & Study Guide
A Woman's High Calling Growth & Study Guide
A Woman's Walk with God Growth & Study Guide

A Woman After God's Own Heart® Bible Study Series

Walking in God's Promises—The Life of Sarah
Cultivating a Life of Character—Judges/Ruth
Becoming a Woman of Beauty & Strength—Esther
Discovering the Treasures of a Godly Woman—Proverbs 31
Nurturing a Heart of Humility—The Life of Mary
Experiencing God's Peace—Philippians
Pursuing Godliness—1 Timothy
Growing in Wisdom & Faith—James
Putting On a Gentle & Quiet Spirit—1 Peter

Children's Books

God's Wisdom for Little Girls—Virtues & Fun from Proverbs 31
God's Wisdom for Little Boys—Character-Building Fun from Proverbs
(co-authored by Jim George)